C000100037

Actual sizes of: a stereoscopic card featuring a view of Worcester from the railway bridge by Earl; a cabinet card of Lucy Francis Fosbury Child (see TB11 on page 16) by Bennett; and a carte-de-visite of an unknown child by Parsons.

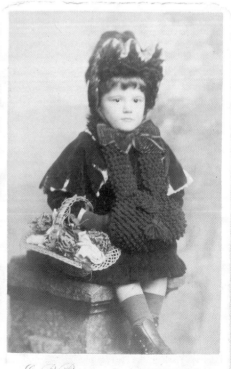

J. Bennett & Sons   WORCESTER & MALVERN

E. P. Parsons   ST NICHOLAS ST. WORCESTER.

PIONEERS OF PHOTOGRAPHY
in the
CITY OF WORCESTER
and around

Ray Jones

PARKBARN

First published in Great Britain in 2007 by
PARKBARN
Martingale Cottage, Church Lane, Hallow, Worcester WR2 6PF

ISBN 978 1 898097 05 1

Typeset by Ray Jones in Baskerville Regular

Printed and bound by Butler and Tanner, Frome, Somerset, England
Cover design by Ray Jones

HS04 The Plough at Tibberton. The licensee was Arthur S. Bowden. A public house named Speed the Plough is now situated on Plough Road and, presumably, is in the same location.

CONTENTS

INTRODUCTION

The earliest known photographic negative in existence was taken by William Henry Fox Talbot in August 1835. This featured an oriel window at Lacock Abbey in Wiltshire. This was the Photogenic Drawing process and from that invention photography developed quickly. Talbot went on to patent a calotype process in 1841 which was to compete directly with the daguerreotype that appeared at about the same time. In the late 1840s Niepce put forward glass as the best base for the negative material. He utilized chemicals that were suspended in albumen. Other developments soon occurred but it was the wet collodion process (of around 1850) that produced a high image quality that encouraged the entrepreneurial efforts of both professional and amateur photographers. To the professional the wet collodion process offered speed of printing which was essential if sales were to be increased to a profitable level. However, the daguerreotype was still very popular and the 1850s was a decade where different processes competed for dominance. Most cartes-de-visite were produced by the wet collodion process. Well-known and enduring firms soon emerged in the 1850s with Thomas Bennett setting up at 46 Foregate Street around 1856, and Francis Charles Earl opening up in rivalry shortly afterwards at 46 Broad Street. These photographers principally worked in their own studios and Victorian families would arrive by appointment dressed in their finest regalia for the event. They were posed with their most serious and respectable expressions much as their ancestors had come to an artist's studio to have their portraits painted. Photography must have seemed a magical and exciting process to those able to afford the recording of family events.

Because early photographs were taken mainly in the studio Victorian examples of everyday life and topographical scenes are few and far between. Fortunately, however, this situation was to change with the invention of the portable camera at the end of the nineteenth century. The Edwardian era saw a rapid expansion in the number of local photographers and they produced a vast array of work which included social events, disasters, sporting occasions, family groups, and nearby landmarks. Particularly popular were views of the

An Edwardian photographic studio. I have never seen a Worcester example so use this image from the studio of West of Cobham. The visible props and fittings seem to be ubiquitous. (JS)

Cathedral, the Commandery, and the riverside. Postcard sending and collecting became an Edwardian craze and the production of postcards became an important source of revenue for many photographers. Early portable cameras were bulky objects and we can only admire the enthusiasm and spirit of the likes of Max Fischer, Percy Parsons, Wilfred Clutterbuck and William Dowty who cycled around town and countryside in search of suitable subjects. They would often submit examples of their work to the *Berrow's Worcester Journal* for possible inclusion in the weekly pictorial supplement (referred to throughout this publication as the *Berrow's Illustrated Supplement*). The first *Berrow's Illustrated Supplement* apparently appeared in January 1909. Acknowledgement of the photographer was usual in the early days of the supplement but within a few years was not as commonplace. I am not sure why this occurred but I do know that some of the unacknowledged featured photographs were the work of Fischer and Colwell.

Photography, however, was not an easy way to make money and many photographers pursued other occupations as well. Arthur J. Neale worked full-time at the Royal Porcelain Works but they allowed him to operate his own photographic studio from his home in Bath Road. Max Fischer had been a commercial printer in Lowesmoor for some years and taking photographs was a natural extension of his activities. Maud Parsons, the wife of Percy Parsons, ran the College Cafe, facing the Cathedral, to supplement their income. My own grandfather, Bertie Dinsdale, worked as a freelance photographer for some time and coupled this with his fresh fish delivery round. Being a photographer in the pioneering years was primarily a way of life and not a licence to print money.

By the outbreak of the Second World War commercial photography was taking on a new face; the staple income for photographers coming from their studio work and commissions for weddings and family events. Newspapers increasingly employed their own photographers although freelance contributions were still sought. The postcard market was less buoyant and was dominated by national firms such as Frith and Salmon. The golden age of the pioneers was effectively over.

Actual photograph sizes are not used in this book but examples of the usual sizes of cartes-de-visite, cabinet cards and stereoscopic cards can be seen on the page opposite the title page. Cartes-de-visite and cabinet cards usually had a reverse design that photographers used in order to advertise their services. Some designs were quite ornate while others were very basic. Some photographers employed a numbering system and I have attempted to analyse this to some extent in the interests of trying to more accurately date individual photographs and also to try to ascertain the approximate output of individual photographers. However much more research is needed in this field.

Mrs Faulkner tries her hand at photography in the grounds of Kempsey House around 1908.

F.R. Logan advertising postcard which probably dates from around 1930. Older bulkier equipment is shown along with the newer lighter and easily portable equipment. The motor car has replaced the Edwardian photographer's bicycle. (JS)

ACKNOWLEDGEMENTS

Thanks are due to the Worcester Record Office (WRO), Jack Stasiak (JS), Chris Garner (CG), Eugene Dinsdale (ED), the late Walter Amphlett (WA), Joy Hall (JH) and Diane Whitehouse (DW) for the use of their material. All of the other photographs and postcards used in this publication are from my own collection. Thanks are also due to: Christopher Garner, the great grandson of Percy Parsons, for details of Percy's life history; Eugene Dinsdale, the son of Bertie Dinsdale, for details of Bertie's life history and to Elizabeth Dowty for permission to use information on W.W. Dowty. Thanks must also be made to Mike Hallett for his original research that made my own research that much easier. The *Berrow's Worcester Journal* and the associated *Berrow's Journal Pictorial Supplements* have been invaluable research sources while the *Memory Lane* articles by Mike Grundy have also been informative.

Right. A portable photographers' platform pictured around 1910. A photographic postcard by Simms of Chipping Norton that reveals the ingenuity of the Edwardian photographers. I am not sure if any Worcester photographers used such a contraption. (JS)

Below. Trimming photographic postcards by Frank Packer of Chipping Norton. Apparently issued as an advertising postcard. (JS)

SURFWORCESTER PHOTOGRAPHIC ARCHIVE

Comprises (example above - a hunt meet at Croome Court by Parsons):

Real and printed photographs of Worcester, Hallow, Grimley, Holt, Shrawley, Great Witley, Witley Court, Abberley, Clifton-On-Teme, Martley, Knightwick, Broadwas, Broadheath, Rushwick, Leigh Sinton, Alfrick, Suckley, Bransford, Powick, Callow End, Kempsey, Norton, Croome, Spetchley, Crowle, Fernhill Heath, Ombersley and areas around. Real photographic rural scenes including hop picking and market gardening.

If you are interested in obtaining good quality photographs for reference, framing, presents and the like then please register your requirements with me. More details are available on the internet:

http://www.surfworcester.co.uk

I am always looking to purchase new material and will pay good prices for interesting postcards and photographs. As a member of the Postcard Traders Association I am always willing to advise on any accumulations of postcards you may have whether they be local, British, or foreign.

OTHER PARKBARN PUBLICATIONS

Unseen Worcester by Ray Jones BA. Comprising 120 A4 pages containing 237 largely unpublished images of the Faithful City. Priced at £11.95.

Porcelain in Worcester 1751-1951: An Illustrated Social History by Ray Jones BA. Comprising 96 A4 pages containing 164 photographs and plans etc. An essential book for anyone interested in Worcester porcelain. Also available from the Porcelain Museum Gift Shop. Priced at £9.95.

Worcester's Lost Theatre - The Story of the Worcester Theatre Royal by Suz Winspear. Comprising 120 A4 pages containing 46 photographs and illustrations. A fascinating book that is of interest to both local residents familiar with the history of Worcester, and theatre buffs eager to learn more about the origins of provincial theatre history. Now priced at only £4.95.

Worcester in Recent Times by Bill Meadows and Geoffrey Hopcraft. Comprising 112 A4 pages containing 235 photographs. An intriguing look at Worcester between the 1940s and 1980s. Refurbished stock only available. Priced at £11.95.

Worcester Past and Present by Ray Jones BA. Comprising 128 pages filled with present-day photographs of the city that are compared with images from the past. Published by Sutton Publishing. Priced at £9.99.

Please email in first instance: ray@surfworcester.co.uk
or contact:
Ray Jones, Martingale Cottage, Church Lane, Hallow, Worcester WR2 6PF
Tel: 01905 640014

E. & F. BALDWIN

Edward and Frank Baldwin first appear in the local directories in 1916 having branches at 24 Mill Street, Kidderminster and 5 The Tything, Worcester (formerly the studios occupied by Terry & Fryer). They later relocated to 12 The Tything. They also had branches dating from earlier at Bath, Cheltenham & Gloucester.

Mrs Barbara Lomas (nee Drew) who features in photograph EB04 used to live at the Worcester branch where her father was the manager/proprietor.

EB01 *Right.* A studio photograph of Diane Jenkins taken on December 12th 1945. Diane is my cousin and Bertie Dinsdale was her grandfather.

EB02 *Below left.* A studio photograph of Eugene Dinsdale taken in 1943. Eugene is my uncle and the youngest son of Bertie Dinsdale.

EB03 *Below right.* A studio photograph of Carole Jones taken around 1948. Carole is my sister and Bertie Dinsdale was her grandfather.

EB04 The Starlight Follies pictured at the Starlight Dancing Academy studio around 1940. It was situated above a flower shop at 16 High Street. From left to right: Mary Harman, Betty Burbidge, Barbara Drew, Rosemary Allbutt, Elsie Andrews and Dorothy Vobe. The discovery of this photograph led to a reunion of several members of the academy in 1995. The academy was run by Miss Gertrude Fisher who according to Mary Inight (nee Harman) was 'a wonderful character and great dance teacher'.

EB05 Walter Whittingham of Cyril Road, Worcester and his trophies which all seem to concern canaries. Walter is holding a prize certificate awarded by the British Canary Association.

THOMAS BENNETT & SON

Thomas Bennett opened at 46 Foregate Street in 1856. He opened a further studio at Gazebo, Church Street, Great Malvern between 1860-1863. However, between 1865-1872 he is listed at 2 Priory Mount, Church Street (Earl had taken over by 1873). Between 1873-1876 he moved from 46 Foregate Street (Earl taking over the studio) to Pierpoint Street and 9 Foregate Street. Thomas was married to Elizabeth and they had four children: Thomas, Robert, Emily and Annie. Thomas had died by 1879 and his son Thomas J. Bennett operated the business from 8 Broad Street as Thomas Bennett and Son (also being known as Bennett's Photographic & Art Studio). The business returned to the studio at Gazebo House, Church Street, Malvern around 1880/1881 (Norman May was in occupation at Gazebo House in 1879 - *Littlebury's Directory of Worcester and District* for 1879). At some stage, possibly around 1888, Robert joined his brother in the business. Bennett definitely produced daguerreotypes at one time but his main legacy is in the field of cartes-de-visite and cabinet cards.

Bennett employed a numbering system for much of his cartes-de-visite and cabinet cards but analysis of his system for dating purposes is not easy as discrepancies do arise with some photographs being un-numbered and others not seeming to be numbered accurately. Bennett did not use a numbering system initially but appeared to be doing so from around the late 1860s. The earliest Broad Street cartes-de-visite I have seen are numbered 11,836a; 12,864 and 16,798 and they make no mention of any premises in Malvern or the relinquished premises in Worcester so logically they should date around 1878 or 1879. However, a later numbered carte-de-visite, No. 19,268 (see TB09), mentions the old premises at Worcester and Great Malvern yet carte-de-visite No. 22,969 mentions Broad Street, Worcester only while carte-de-visite No. 24,596 (see TB08) should actually date from earlier as it advertises the 46 Foregate Street premises and the first

TB01 Ellen Elizabeth Amphlett (1829-1903). One of Bennett's earliest cartes-de-visite probably taken at his Foregate Street studio around 1860/62. (WA)

TB02 The reverse of the carte-de-visite featuring Ellen Elizabeth Amphlett. No numbering process is evident. (WA)

Malvern premises used by Bennett. Cartes-de-visite Nos. 37,526; 37,546 and 37,775 are dated 1886, No. 50,830 is dated 1888, while No. 53,017 is dated 1889. Strangely I have a cabinet card No. 5327 and dated 1889 - possibly a digit is missing as No. 53,270 or similar would make more sense. Other post 1879 cabinet cards are numbered far higher (44,019, 79,534, 95,774 and 114,216). Care must therefore be taken when trying to date Bennett or Bennett & Son(s) cartes-de-visite and research is on-going.

From all this, rather haphazard, information it would appear that the business was producing around three to five thousand cartes-de-visite and cabinet cards per year. Several advertisements help to increase our knowledge of the business:

An advertisement in *Kelly's Directory* for 1863 states that Bennett charges five shillings per six cartes-de-visite and also offers sizes of work from stereo size to 23 inches x 19 inches.

In *Littlebury's Directory of Worcester and District* for 1879, T.J. Bennett advertises (opposite Postal Regulations on page 58) as follows:

'PORTRAITS. In every variety of style and size, including the beautiful and popular Rembrandts - the lighting in the New Studio giving the most perfect results. In building the Studio at 8 Broad Street, every care has been taken to make it as complete as possible by applying all the latest improvements in lighting and situation, which, combined with the late THOMAS BENNETT'S experience, has resulted in a Studio leaving nothing to be desired. Special attention has been given in the construction of the new premises to provide convenient waiting and dressing rooms. T.J. Bennett hopes for a continuance of the patronage so liberally accorded to his late father.

Landscape and Architectural Photography, embracing views of Mansions, Churches, Schools, Gardens, Groups etc.

PORTRAITS ENLARGED to any size and painted in oil or water colour.

Old photographs and glass pictures copied, the best results guaranteed.

A large assortment of Cathedral and Local Views, Portraits of Celebrities, etc., to select from.

Framing, Gilding, etc., done in best and cheapest style, and Orders executed with despatch.'

In the booklet *Worcester the Faithful City* published in 1897 there is a good description of the business:

'Just over forty years ago, when photography was regarded more as a scientific plaything than as the most wonderful discovery of the age, the firm of Messrs. T. Bennett & Sons, established their studio in the grey old Cathedral city, and commenced practice in taking 'likenesses,' as they were then termed, by the new process of the daguerreotype. During the intervening period what marvellous progress has been made.

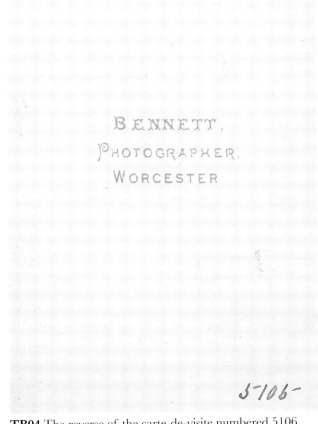

TB03 Another one of Bennett's earliest cartes-de-visite (numbered 5106) probably taken at his Foregate Street studio in the 1860s.

TB04 The reverse of the carte-de-visite numbered 5106.

Improvement has followed improvement with each succeeding decade, and the application of photography to science, art, and industry, may be almost said to have reached its culminating point of development in the discovery of the 'X' Ray, or Rontgen process, which has unfolded the secrets of nature with startling and marvellous effect. Steadily following in the path of progress and improvement, Messrs. T. Bennett & Sons have attained a premier position in their art, and a high professional reputation of far wider than local significance. Their handsome studios, centrally situated at 8 Broad Street, between the Cross and Severn Bridge, present an attractive window frontage utilised for an effective exhibition of artistic specimens of portraits of Royal and distinguished celebrities, views of buildings, and objects of interest in the locality, both architectural and historical. The interior arrangements include reception rooms, replete with every comfort and convenience for sitters awaiting their turn. This apartment is liberally embellished with highly finished pictures by the bromide, carbon, platino-type, and silver point processes, in enlargements, re-produced from original portraits, or smaller copies of photographs, illustrating all the latest improvements in scientific photography. The studio proper is a large and splendidly-lighted apartment, completely equipped with all the most recent improvements in apparatus and appliances for the execution of high-class work, from the smallest vignette miniature to the handsome three-quarters or full length presentment of some civic magnate. The accessories provided for taking groups or arranging a suitable background for various styles of pictures desired by sitters, are of the most complete description, enabling the operator to select the details of the surroundings in appropriate harmony with the subject or individual photographed. Thoroughly finished and accomplished experts in the difficult arts of posing and arrangement are retained, and by the aid of the instantaneous process, complete fidelity of expression, and the most natural presentments are obtained in every detail of the portrait. The perfection attained in the case of children's portraits is a noteworthy feature of Messrs. T. Bennett & Son's skilful practice, and another difficult branch of work is specialised in animal and landscape reproduction. In addition to the various departments of photography already indicated, the members of the firm produce some exceedingly well executed oil paintings, both landscape and portrait, which are submitted for inspection at the studios, and evidence the fact that Messrs. Bennett are perfectly competent to hold their own in the higher regions of executive art.

The firm have received from time to time flattering recognition of their excellent productions from the highest sources, as evidenced by the following communications:-

BALMORAL.: Sir Henry Ponsonby is commanded by the Queen to thank Messrs. Bennett & Sons for the excellent photographs of the two ceremonies connected with the Worcester Jubilee Statue.'

(Similar 'thank you' letters were also received from Sandringham, and St. James' Palace.)

The business of Thomas Bennett and Son had probably been very profitable (the 1881 census shows that they could afford a servant) but possibly began to slowly decline after the death of Thomas. Neither of his sons (Thomas, born around 1853 in Cambridgeshire, and Robert, who was four years younger) displayed quite the same level of business acumen and they were rumoured to be rather too fond of the demon drink. Michael Dowty stated that 'one died in circumstances that were never satisfactorily explained, whilst the other took an extreme measure of potassium cyanide, a year later, in the first floor room over the shop'. Michael's father, William Ward Dowty, was to purchase the Bennett business on February 25th 1913.

TB05 Carte-de-visite of Jane Amphlett of Northingtown. She was born in 1822. (WA)

TB06 Rear side of the carte-de-visite of Jane Amphlett which probably dates it to the mid 1860s. This carte-de-visite back can also be found without the Church Street address and therefore the basic design was used by Bennett prior to 1860-63. (WA)

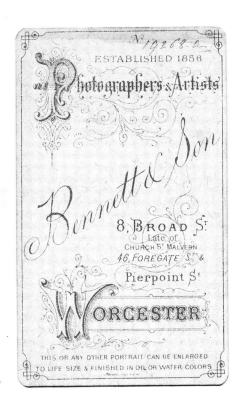

TB07 Another early carte-de-visite (numbered m937) probably taken at his Great Malvern studio in the early 1870s.

TB08 Reverse of carte-de-visite numbered 24,596. (No. m937 also uses the same back design). The design was used earlier than that of TB09 yet the hand numbering suggests otherwise.

TB09 The reverse of a carte-de-visite numbered 19268a.

TB10 A superb study of a cricket team possibly around 1890. Unfortunately this large photograph (11.75 inches x 9.5 inches) is not captioned.

TB11 & TB12 Lucy Francis Fosbury Child who was born around 1874. She was probably about 15 years old when this photograph was taken. It is numbered 53,412a which also suggests a dating of around 1889. Bennett & Son had become Bennett & Sons around 1888/9.

TB13 Rear side of a cabinet card numbered 114,216 which is the latest numbering I have seen. This design was also used for both the cabinet cards below.

TB14 Cabinet card numbered 44,019. The reverse design is as per TB13 but advertises Bennett & Son and so dates from around 1887.

TB15 Cabinet card numbered 79,534.

Worcester Electric Tramway Siege, 1903=4.

T. Bennett & Sons, Photographers,
Worcester and Malvern.

TB16 & TB17 There are currently 15 known different postcards published by Bennett & Sons featuring the Worcester Electric Tramway Siege. Unfortunately they were printed rather than real photographic postcards so the detail is somewhat hazy.

TB18 The Broad Street shop as it appeared in *Worcester the Faithful City* - an advertising booklet published in 1897. (WRO)

Worcester Electric Tramway Siege, 1903.

Bennett & Sons, Photographers,
Worcester and Malvern.

TB19 A fine photographic postcard of The Cross featuring a view that dates to around 1885. Shortly afterwards St. Swithin's Street was widened and the business of Goldring, pastry cook, moved a short distance to 22 The Cross. A good example of Bennett & Sons 'archive' range whereby Thomas and Robert Bennett produced as real photographic postcards views of Worcester taken in the late Victorian period. Other examples may be seen in *Unseen Worcester* - notably photograph Nos. 155 & 156 featuring the floods of May 1886.

TB20 The Cross, Worcester on a real photographic postcard postally used in 1912.

MR. HAROLD ELVERSTON.

MR. EDWARD GOULDING.

TB21 & TB22 Harold Elverston, the Liberal candidate and Edward Goulding, the Conservative & Unionist candidate. They were the two protagonists in the by-election held at Worcester in 1908 (see pages 133-139).

TB23 A postcard of a military procession in Church Street, Malvern that shows the Malvern premises of Bennetts at Gazebo House (photographer unknown).

WALTER J. BROWN

Brown was initially based at 46 Foregate Street from around 1888-1890. This had been the studio previously occupied by A. & G. Taylor. Brown soon moved to premises at 9 Bridge Street, Worcester (1890-1892) but his venture into photography appeared to be relatively short-lived.

WB01 *Right.* A Foregate Street studio carte-de-visite (some water damage).

WB02 *Below left.* A Bridge Street studio carte-de-visite.

WB03 *Below right.* The reverse of a Bridge Street cabinet card.

W. J. BROWN, 46, FOREGATE ST
WORCESTER.

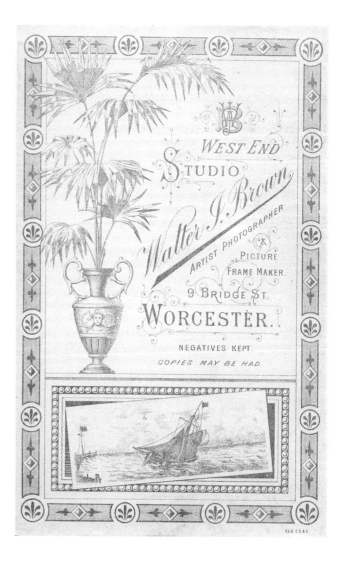

HENRY E. BURCHELL

Burchell operated from his home at *Elford* 65 Park Avenue, Worcester. Burchell was a relatively unknown photographer and was possibly mainly a keen amateur who used photography as a method of making some extra money. He appeared to be mainly active in the late 1920s and 1930s.

HB01 A group of local firemen.

HB02 John Bee was the organist at the opening of the Gaumont cinema in the mid 1930s; he then became manager and organist during the war years. Here he is sat at his 'Mighty Illuminated Compton' on which he played stirring tunes as a prelude to the films. Bee was appointed as manager of the new Odeon cinema in 1950. He retired in 1963 at the age of 66, and died in 1983 at the age of 87. He was a popular local personality who had won the Military Cross during the First World War.

JOHN J. CAM

John James Cam (1850-1919) is better known as one of Worcester's leading Victorian industrialists (he ran the Cam Engineering Works that was based in Charles Street) but he was also a well-known amateur photographer. He was a founder member of the Worcester Photographic Survey Society which, I believe, was the forerunner of the Worcester Camera Club.

JC01 The Queen Elizabeth House pictured in a sorry looking state prior to its removal to the Trinity in 1891.

Cam was a keen cyclist which enabled him to travel around the local countryside capturing views for posterity. Apparently he was a founder member of the Worcester Tricycle Club who had several enthusiastic pioneering photographers. The club had its own camera section which held occasional events in order to show off members photographic efforts.

JC02 *Above.* Fladbury Mill around 1888.

JC03 *Below.* A Knightwick panorama around 1888.

WILFRED T. CLUTTERBUCK

Wilfred (possibly Wilfrid) Thomas Clutterbuck first appeared in the local directories in 1904. He operated from his home at *Sabbatta* 29 Bozward Street, St. John's from around 1904-1910. He was then based at *Brighton Villas* 181/182 Henwick Road for a short time before moving to Evesham during 1911. There is also a Frederick Clutterbuck listed at 181 Henwick Road in the *Kelly's Directory* for 1912 so perhaps he was temporarily staying with one of his relatives.

Clutterbuck did not sign his postcards but fortunately he contributed to the *Berrow's Illustrated Supplement* and thus I have been able to identify many examples of his work. His work often appeared in the supplements from 1909 onwards. They were mainly hunt, wedding, football club and local event photographs. Areas he covered included Bromsgrove, the Teme valley, Hanley Swan, Croome, and Upton Snodsbury. An interesting contribution he made was a photograph of the 'Wychbold fat boy' - he weighed 15 stones at the age of eleven - on May 8th 1909. Other contributions included the Hallow gardening class (August 28th 1909), the first hop pickers at Leigh (September 11th 1909) and roasting two sheep for hop pickers (October 1st 1910). He made no more contributions from his Worcester address after May 18th 1912. He subsequently moved to Evesham where he continued his photographic business from 51 Port Street, Bengeworth (*Kelly's Directory* for 1921). However the *Kelly's Directories* for 1924-1940 list him as a confectioner. A solitary contribution was made to the *Berrow's Illustrated Supplement* on June 26th 1926 which featured Worcestershire fruit growers on a tour of the Vale of Evesham.

A great speciality of Clutterbuck was to follow the hunts and capture various scenes of their meets. Hunt meets were a very important social activity at this time and the *Berrow's Journal* reported on them in some detail - even including all the names of the participants. Clutterbuck's hunt photographs were thus an ideal feature for the supplements. Fischer and Parsons increased their coverage of local meets after Clutterbuck's departure for Evesham.

CL01 A meet at Abberley which dates from around 1909.

CL02 This meet scene at Great Witley dates from around 1908. On the right is the old school while in the distance is Witley chapel.

CL03 A similar scene outside the Hundred House, Great Witley. This photograph featured in the *Berrow's Illustrated Supplement* of March 20th 1909.

CL04 Local children assembled together at the meet at Hallow Green. This postcard photograph appeared in the *Berrow's Illustrated Supplement* of March 11th 1911. This was Clutterbuck's last acknowledged contribution for some fourteen months. He made two further contributions in 1912 covering Abbots Morton and Ombersley and then, presumably, left for Evesham.

CL05 The meet at Hallow Green during the winter of 1909. This photograph featured in the *Berrow's Illustrated Supplement* of March 20th 1909.

CL06 The meet outside the Red Lion at Holt Heath probably during the winter of 1908/1909.

CL07 The meet outside Ombersley Court during the winter of 1908/1909. This postcard photograph appeared in the *Berrow's Illustrated Supplement* of January 30th 1909.

CL08 & CL09 The meet outside the Royal Oak, Broadwas probably around 1910.

CL10 The meet at Severn Stoke probably around 1910.

CL11 Witley Choir Presentation. This postcard photograph appeared in the *Berrow's Illustrated Supplement* of June 26th 1909.

CL12 Bransford scene captured around 1909. This is the road that leads to Smith End Green and Suckley and so this part of the village is still a relatively quiet backwater.

CL13 The station at Bransford Road around 1909. The station was some distance from the main village, being close to the Bear and Ragged Staff.

CL14 Hylton Road in flood during December 1910. As Clutterbuck lived locally gaining access to the flood activity was not a problem for him. Clutterbuck would have taken this photograph from somewhere near the junction of Hylton Road and Chequers Lane. The view shows the eastern side of the Hylton Road nearest the river. Another Clutterbuck flood photograph, taken at roughly the same spot and time, can be seen in *Unseen Worcester* on page 79 (No. 157). A Max Fischer photograph of this flood is on page 81 (MF22).

CL15 Tramway Staff Kit Inspection at the tramway depot, St. John's, Worcester. Now the site of the Co-operative supermarket. This postcard photograph appeared in the *Berrow's Illustrated Supplement* of June 18th 1910.

CL16 Orphan Sunday. The Railwaymen's Widows and Orphans Fund Church Parade Committee and Officers. Submitted to the *Berrow's Illustrated Supplement* by Clutterbuck (July 30th 1910). The photograph was taken in Trinity Street looking towards St. Nicholas Street. This view has now changed completely.

CL17 The Maypole Dance at Himbleton Fete probably around 1910.

CL18 Clutterbuck had left Worcester for Evesham when this photograph was taken in a Worcestershire garden. The postcard was used by him personally and sent from Upton Snodsbury on May 10th 1912. He writes to the secretary and organiser of the Bishampton Church Parade in order to inform him or her that he will be attending the event in order to take photographs.

A. & G. COLWELL

George Colwell was born around 1864 in Wiltshire and is listed as a photographer in the 1901 census. He appears in the local directories from around 1908 onwards. George was a Quaker and his home - *Greenhill Villa* was formerly a Quaker school. The photographic work was carried out in the cellar of his large seven bedroomed house. A speciality of his work was hop yard photography. His bike was especially adapted in order to cope with the bulk of his camera and photographic equipment. His wife often accompanied him on his journeys. His work often appeared in the *Berrow's Illustrated Supplement* from around 1910 onwards.

His abilities were not just confined to photography; the late Ronald Bick (George Colwell was his stepfather) told me that he invented rubber mudguards for lorries. I then found further evidence of this in the *Berrow's Illustrated Supplement* of June 30th 1923 which has a photograph of the testing of Mr G. Colwell's 'Anti-Mud Splash Guard'. *Berrow's Journal* reported that the guard consisted 'of a strong piece of sheet steel fitted by bolts near the wheels and to which was attached a square of pure rubber to catch the mud'. Apparently the device performed well in a demonstration at Croft Road and the RAC were suitably impressed.

Colwell continued to be listed as a photographer in the directories until 1936. George must have been a reasonably affluent and benevolent man as he bought Mr Bick his first car!

His brother, Frederick Herbert, was a second-hand bookseller with premises at 56 Sidbury (possibly selling the work of his brother).

A John Colwell was listed as a photographer at *Greenhill Villa*, London Road, Worcester between 1904 and 1908 and he may have been the father of George (he was also listed as a second-hand bookseller in Pump Street in 1896).

GC01 A Primrose League visit that was featured in the *Berrow's Illustrated Supplement* of October 14th 1909. Colwell may have had Conservative leanings for he made the long journey down to Wargrave Hall in Berkshire with the Executive Council and Wardens of the Primrose League. Wargrave Hall was the home of Edward Goulding who can be seen on the front row, second from the right. Goulding is also featured on page 19 [TB22], page 78 [MF16] & pages 133-139.

GC02 A spectacular butchers shopfront. Unfortunately the name of the butchers is not apparent.

GC03 Owen's bus service from Worcester to Pensax, Abberley and Witley. AB3657 is pictured at Five Ways by the Norwich Union offices of Watkins and Sayce.

GC04 & GC05 Two local weddings photographed by Colwell that probably date from the First World War period. My great aunt, Emily Jones, attended both events but, alas, she did not record whose weddings they were. She is pictured above: top row, third from left, and below: middle row, third from right. She is also pictured on page 58 (HD02).

GC06 & GC07 Saint Catherine's Hill, London Road, Worcester was a large house set amidst spacious grounds. This was the home of the Reverend Edward Gilliat in 1908. Part of the grounds were used for the construction, around 1910, of the new St. Martin's church. During the First World War the house was temporarily used to accommodate Belgian refugees. Colwell was commissioned to take the family photograph shown above while below he attended a fete held in the grounds. It was possibly the Worcester Brotherhood Fete that was held annually at Saint Catherine's Hill but there does seem to be a shortage of male attenders in this photograph. The Worcester Brotherhood Fete held at Saint Catherine's Hill in 1913 can be seen on page 80 (MF20).

GC08 & GC09 Two rare examples of oversized postcards produced by Colwell.

Above. Crowds gather outside the Cathedral during the celebrations for the proclamation of King George V.

Left. Revellers at Hanbury Fair.

GC10 A charming group of tennis players. I wonder where the photograph was taken and who is pictured?

GC11 The NALGO Whist Drive held in the Council Chambers, Shirehall during February 1914.

GC12 An idyllic river Severn scene which I suspect was taken in the Bevere area.

GC13 The Holt Fleet Hotel was a major destination for local holidaymakers. The steamer is the Avonmore and the date is around 1909.

GC14 Early motor car at the Holt Fleet Hotel around 1909. The trippers had probably driven down from the Black Country.

GC15 Motor action at Shelsley Walsh around 1910. AB781 waits for the signal to start. Two similar photographs by Colwell appeared in my book *Worcestershire at Work* (now out of print) on pages 120/121.

The Stanford area was a favourite of Colwell and he photographed many views in this area of the Teme valley. His main competitor in this area was possibly Wedley of Stourport who predominated in nearby Abberley.

      GC16 Stanford Bridge showing the post office in the foreground. Next door is the Stanford Bridge Hotel.

      GC17 Stanford Fete Baby Show. This photograph featured in the *Berrow's Illustrated Supplement* of July 2nd 1910.

GC18 The Martley Foresters Procession at Martley. The building in the background is Rectory Cottage. Photograph taken around 1910.

GC19 A superbly posed quality view of hop pickers by a crib. Photograph taken around 1910. In 1906, according to the *Berrow's Worcester Journal*, 3,672 acres were under hop cultivation in Worcestershire (Herefordshire - 6,500 acres).

GC20 Hop workers in the fields of James and William H. Leeke, Great House Farm, Leigh.

GC21 Floods were an occasional hazard at Leeke's. This photograph featured in the *Berrow's Illustrated Supplement* of September 7th 1912.

GC22 A house that still exists on the main Worcester to Tenbury Wells road, close to Great Witley. Postcard postally used in 1904.

GC23 An unidentified boy, probably a rural location.

GC24 A tranquil unidentified rural scene.

GC25 & GC26 Colwell also visited the Worcestershire Imperial Yeomanry camps held at Eastnor. Percy Parsons and Tilleys of Ledbury also took photographs at these camps which I believe were sometimes held at Croome and Witley Court.

W. H. COX

Cox was based in Wichenford and his postcard views that I have seen encompass the Hallow, Sinton Green and Clifton areas. Those postally used range between 1938-1942. He was active as early as 1932 as a photograph of Barbourne Cricket Club that appeared in the *Berrow's Illustrated Supplement* of that year bears his name.

COX01 & COX02 Classic views of Hallow in the 1930s.

COX03 The Steps Farm, Clifton. The postcard was postally used on August 6th 1940 but the sender is unconcerned by the war: 'Here I am having a lovely time. The countryside is glorious, also the weather. Each morning I have been weeding in my shorts & am getting brown. Last evening we went up to the vicarage to play bowls. I quite enjoyed it, very restful after hockey'.

COX04 A bus bound for Worcester pictured in the heart of Clifton village.

BERTIE C. DINSDALE

My own grandfather, Bertie Charles Dinsdale (1877-1951), worked for Fox and Co. in The Tything from around 1890. He had left St. George's School at the age of twelve but had temporarily returned in order to help assist with the new input of female pupils. Bertie often walked through The Tything and found the window displays of Fox and Co. fascinating and one day the curious manager asked him why this was so. Bertie impressed the manager, Harry Proud, with his enthusiasm and on finding out that Bertie could ride a bicycle promptly offered him a job. Initially Bertie helped in a general capacity but he eventually became a fully fledged photographer. One of his more bizarre tasks was to photograph inmates at the prison in Castle Street. Included among these was the last man to be executed at Worcester in 1919. He was a Chinese man who had been found guilty of murdering another of his own race in Warley Woods.

During the First World War Bertie's contribution to the war effort was a stint at the Armstrong Siddeley factory in Birmingham that was making tank shells etc. He lodged with relatives in Birmingham and only returned to Worcester at the weekends. Around 1919 Fox and Co. ceased trading for various reasons (see page 83). They were unable to pay off Bertie in full so, as part of his pay off, they gave him his German-made camera. The camera, tripod and plate glass case were fairly hefty items and Bertie had to especially adapt his bicycle to transport them around. This enabled Bertie to work as a freelance photographer for around three years. His chief work encompassed Saturday weddings, hunting parties, and local political activities. His photographs were also used in election literature. Bertie coupled this work with his fresh fish delivery round (while he had been working in Birmingham he had picked up information about how to buy fish at the wholesale market and resell to the public).

Unfortunately the work of Bertie was destroyed when he kindly donated his old glass plates to a member of the family for use as cloches in his back garden! Bertie did not, apparently, sign his work so the only evidence I have of his work are family photographs and the items he contributed to the *Berrow's Illustrated Supplement*.

BD01 May Woodhouse and her mother, Catherine. Bertie met his future wife while working at Fox and Co. May and her mother were both working for the Armstrong family (the well-known firm of drapers and outfitters based in Sansome Walk) as household staff in 1904. May was employed as an assistant cook and waitress while Catherine was head cook. The Armstrong's home was then at *Eastbourne Lodge* 51 Britannia Square. A requirement for the staff was to have their photograph taken so that the butler would know they were staff members and therefore allowed access to the house. Fox and Co. were nearby and thus Bertie took this cabinet sized photograph. Romance then blossomed for Bertie and May and they were to marry in the summer of 1906.

BD02 The wedding of Bertie and May at Felton church, Herefordshire on July 9th 1906. Back row, left to right: William Woodhouse, Auntie Kitty, Albert Dinsdale [best man], Bertie, May, Albert Woodhouse [bride's father], Mr Green, -?-. Front row: Auntie Bessie, flower girl [on grass], Ethel Dinsdale [bridesmaid], Lilian Dinsdale [bridesmaid], Mary Woodhouse, flower girl [on grass], Jim Wood. Bertie actually took the photograph himself. The grave digger, Mr Treasure, was commandeered to remove and replace the cap on the Fox owned camera with Bertie secretly indicating to him the end of the six second exposure time.

BD03 A family photograph dating from 1913, probably taken in the back yard of their Pinkett Street home. From left to right: May, Albert Woodhouse (father of May Beatrice Dinsdale), Mary Woodhouse (grandmother of May Beatrice Dinsdale), Cecil (on lap of Mary Woodhouse), May Beatrice Dinsdale, Mary (on her mother's lap), Bertie, Albert and Amelia.

BD04 The funeral of the late Mr Tustin of Worcester - the wreaths and his favourite horse, Silver (*Berrow's Illustrated Supplement* - July 18th 1914). Please note that the quality of BD04, BD05 and BD06 are affected by the fact that they are copied from the original printed *Berrow's Illustrated Supplements* and so are not photographic items. (WRO)

ENTERTAINMENT AT ST. STEPHEN'S, WORCESTER.   FLOWER GIRLS AND HUNTING BOYS.
(Photo B. C. Dinsdale, 8, Pinkett Street.)

BD05 St. Stephen's School entertainments (*Berrow's Illustrated Supplement* - February 28th 1914). (WRO)

BD06 Three family members prepare for their war duties. (*Berrow's Illustrated Supplement* - October 31st 1914). Bertie's only other contribution featured an Infirmary romance that led to a Whitsuntide wedding (May 29th 1915). (WRO)

SERGT. WILLIAMSON. OF THE WORCESTERSHIRE YEOMANRY, AND HIS TWO SONS
(BARRY STREET, WORCESTER). (Photo Dinsdale, Pinkett Street, Worcester.)

WILLIAM W. DOWTY

William Ward Dowty (1887-1979), purchased the established Bennett business on February 25th 1913. Unfortunately this coincided with the death of his own father, William Dowty (proprietor of the Abbey Pharmacy in Pershore), and a difficult period for William Ward followed as he struggled to both attend to matters at home and to kick-start his newly acquired business. Much of William Ward's early business years were spent cycling around the Pershore areas where he took many photographic postcard views that were sold in local shops. Private work for families plus the occasional newsworthy happening in the local press were other aspects of his work. Contributions to the *Berrow's Illustrated Supplement* were made from the summer of 1910 onwards, initially mainly covering events in the Pershore area. Most of his photographs were taken on Thornton Pickard or Sanderson half-plate cameras. His son, the late Michael Dowty, recalled that they were not the easiest of cameras to use but they did produce memorable results in the capable and experienced hands of WWD.

Michael, a renowned local and national photographer, fondly remembered his days at the Broad Street premises in his book *Worcester in Old Photographs* (Alan Sutton Publishing Ltd., - first published in 1986):

'I grew up at 8 Broad Street in the 30s and 40s, at a time when there was no great shame in "living on the premises". Several of our business neighbours did likewise, finding that it made sound economical and practical sense. Our own domestic and working accommodation were both excellent and spacious, with splendid panoramic views of the city from the fourth floor (better still for those brave enough to climb on the roof). From the lower windows we were able to study everyday city life and watch the carnivals, military parades and other passing events, including the hill-climb competitors heading for Shelsley Walsh. Internally a steady flow of pedestrian traffic made its way to and from the studio: portrait sitters, pedigree pet owners, the inventor with his latest brainchild, ballroom dancers and their trophies, and wedding parties laying confetti trails as liberal as the scatterings of "hares" in a paper-chase. The variety was endless.'

William Ward served with the Royal Artillery in France during the later stages of the First World War. Subsequently he was rarely seen without his 'Gunners' tie and British Legion badge. Like most of his professional contemporaries, William Ward was primarily a portrait and wedding photographer. He took his work seriously but had a sense of humour as well. The business continued to prosper after the end of the Second World War. In 1956 the shop was closed down by WWD and he and his son, Michael, then continued in the business from home.

WWD01 Pershore Fruit Market Committee around 1908. The photograph was taken in Broad Street, a short distance from the chemists shop of the Dowtys', which was situated in the High Street. Many of WWD's early postcards and photographs were taken in and around the Pershore area. This aspect of WWD's work was comprehensively covered in Michael Dowty's book *Around Pershore in Old Photographs.* (Alan Sutton Publishing Ltd., - first published in 1988).

WWD02 & WWD03 Typical studio portraits from the Pershore days.

WWD04 A busy Pershore Fruit Market, around 1908. Possibly taken on the same day as WWD01.

53

WWD05 Worcestershire Yeomanry Ball held on January 11th 1912. The writer has sent this photographic postcard as a Valentines Day card - perhaps not that romantic!

WWD06 A military and civilian group pose in the grounds of Pershore Abbey.

WWD07 Peopleton Band around 1908. Peopleton church is in the background.
WWD08 *Below left*. Ernie Payne, champion cyclist at a Pershore Show.
WWD09 *Below right*. King George VI and the Mayor of Worcester outside the Guildhall.

WWD10 & WWD11 Cottages at Broughton and a fine country house. Can anyone pin down the exact locations and do the buildings still exist?

WWD12 Charlton Post Office around 1908.

WWD13 Broad Street, Worcester. Dowty's premises were near The Cross so are not visible in this view. However, just to the right of the various carts are the premises of Horace Dudley at 46 Broad Street. This was No. 18 in a series (perhaps WWD's first Worcester series of views after his arrival in Broad Street in 1913).

HORACE H. DUDLEY

Horace H. Dudley had branches in many places including West Bromwich, Kettering, Stoke, Leicester, and Crewe. They took over the former Earl studios at 46 Broad Street around 1908 and had a presence in Worcester for many years. They appear to have been mainly portrait and wedding artists. Many of my old family photographs appear to have been taken at the Dudley studios. Their low prices and promotional activities made them very popular with the citizens of Worcester.

Opposite page. Early examples (before and during the First World War) from the Worcester studio.

HD01 *Opposite page, top left.* Harriet Jones (nee Whitehouse) was born in 1853 and married in 1876.

HD02 *Opposite page, top right.* Miss Emily Jones (1890-1967) was Harriet's third child. Emily (see page 36) was my father's aunt while Harriet was my great grandmother.

HD03 *Opposite page, bottom left.* A Hammond of Lulsley family photograph dating from around the First World War (see pages 118-119).

HD04 *Opposite page, bottom right.* Bessie and Edward Hayward (see photograph PF04 on page 107).

Later examples (1920s and 1930s) from the studio.

HD05 *Left.* A Dinsdale trio - from the left: Doris Jones (1921-2000), Irene Porter (1918-1997), and Howard Dinsdale (1923-2000). This 'cardette portrait' photograph was taken in 1925.

HD06 *Above.* Doris Dinsdale, my late mother, at the age of 17 in a photograph from around 1938.

HD07 *Below left.* Another Dinsdale trio - from the left: Joyce Room (born 1928), Eugene (born 1931), and Gladys Shuck (born 1928) pictured in 1933.

HD08 *Below.* George Jones (1921-1991), my father, at the age of 21 in a photograph from around 1942.

59

FRANCIS C. EARL

The main competitor to Thomas Bennett in Worcester during Victorian times was Francis Charles Earl. He was born about 1828 and married Dorcas Millward. They had a son, Francis Ferdinand, who was christened at All Saints church on 26 December 1868. Earl was based at 46 Broad Street from 1860 to 1892. Around 1873 he took over the studios at 46 Foregate Street and 2 Priory Mount, Church Street, Malvern (both from Thomas Bennett). He relinquished the Malvern studio in the early 1880s (by 1884 Norman May was running the studio). *Owen's Directory* of 1881 mentions a branch at Stourbridge. From 1900 to 1903 the firm operated under the name of Earl and Company at 12 Severn Terrace, Worcester. Francis died in December 1903. Various advertisements help us plot Earl's career:

In the *Worcester Calendar* for 1865 Earl advertised 'the new patented Diamond Cameo Portrait' at a cost of 10 shillings per dozen.

In the *Malvern Directory* for 1865 he advertises his 'views of Malvern' in 'cabinet, carte, and stereoscopic sizes'.

In *Littlebury's Directory of the City of Worcester* for 1869 Earl made the following claims:

'F.C. Earl, 46 Broad Street, Worcester, Photographic Artist, Begs to announce that he is now producing Instantaneous Photographs of Children, with their home-like natural surrounding; and that he has extensive Premises which afford facilities for grouping large numbers of persons; with the advantage of Two Studios which enables him readily to produce in-door or outdoor effects.

Enlargements to Life-Size. For this purpose Mr. E. is supplied with the best arrangement for ARTIFICIAL LIGHT, in addition to the SOLAR CAMERA, so that he is prepared to execute work in this direction with-out delay caused by the absence of Sun; and he constantly produces large Pictures, FINISHED IN OIL OR WATER COLOURS, OR CRAYON, from faded or inferior Originals, in every case guaranteeing a successful resemblance.

Portraits of Animals are effectively produced in this manner, as a variety of examples will aptly prove.

PHOTO—CRAYON PORTRAITS: A new and pleasing style, combining the delicacy and exactitude of the Photograph with the brilliancy and masterly touch of the most artistically executed Drawing in Chalk.

LANDSCAPE AND ARCHITECTURAL PHOTOGRAPHY is made a Specialite of and the Advertiser possesses Negatives of most Objects of interest throughout the County.'

In *Littlebury's Directory of Worcester & District* for 1873 Earl's advertisement included:

'CABINET PORTRAITS - this new and elegantly proportioned portrait is most carefully studied in regard to its artistic arrangement and chaste appointment.'

In Littlebury's Directory for Worcester & District for 1879 Earl made the following claims:

'F.C. Earl believes that his PHOTOGRAPHIC PORTRAITURE will be found equal to the productions of Foreign Studios at Prices which must be considered strictly moderate.

LANDSCAPE PHOTOGRAPHY is especially studied, and a staff of Artists can at all times be despatched at an hour's notice.

Instantaneous Portraits of Children.'

FE01 & FE02 Two early examples of scenic cartes-de-visite. I am fairly certain that they are of Raglan castle. They date from around 1875 and are numbered 2451 and 2456.

Analysis of the cartes-de-visite numbering system used by Earl is problematical. Some are un-numbered and it is difficult to know if his landscape views were numbered separately from his portrait views (I suspect they were). The highest numbered carte-de-visite I have seen is No. 68,361 so this gives a rough estimate of a production of nearly 2,000 different cartes-de-visite per year over his career. I rather think that the actual figure was probably nearer 3,000 per year since No. 60,890 (FE13) should logically date to around 1883 (Earl apparently had no presence in Great Malvern after 1884 but there is always the likelihood that Earl would use up his old stock of blank cartes). Research is on-going.

Earl also dealt in photographic apparatus and chemicals. The local firm of Deighton and Co., booksellers and stationers, who were based at 53 High Street, stocked a range of Earl's local landscape views. Earl was undoubtedly a good photographer and a canny businessman.

FE03 The F.C. Earl studios at 46 Foregate Street (formerly the premises of Thomas Bennett). This photograph dates from between 1876 and 1884. Earl was not at this location for long (interestingly none of his work that I have seen advertises the Foregate Street address) and he had moved from the premises by 1884 when Alexander and George Taylor were in situ. William J. Brown was also at this location in 1888 but by the early 1890s the site was required for the new Victoria Institute which was to open in 1896. (WRO)

FE04 *Above left.* Carte-de-visite of Judith Perrins of Worcester numbered 3594. A Judith Perrins died locally in December 1865.

FE05 *Above right.* Carte-de-visite of Mr. Perrins of Worcester numbered 6920. There is a reasonable chance that there is some connection to the Perrins family of *Worcestershire Sauce* fame but I have so far been unable to pin this down with any certainty.

FE06 Carte-de-visite of a member of the Amphlett family numbered 3968 (see FE09). She was once thought to be Anne Amphlett (1813-1844) but this photograph was taken many years after her death and this lady bears a close resemblance to Ellen Elizabeth Amphlett (see TB01 on page 12). However she also bears a close resemblance to another lady in the Amphlett family album who was also called Ellen and who was also born in 1829. This Ellen married Richard Gardner of *The Parsonage*, Ombersley and died in 1895. Consequently it is difficult to say who this lady is with any certainty. The carte-de-visite would appear to date from around 1862. Note the backdrop of Worcester Cathedral that Earl evidently used. (WA)

FE07 *Above left*. Carte-de-visite of William Amphlett of Dunhampton (second son of William Amphlett of Northingtown) numbered 5564. He was born in 1824 and died in 1889. (WA)

FE08 *Above right*. Carte-de-visite of Jane Elizabeth Roe (wife of William Amphlett) numbered 5565. She died in 1899. (WA)

FE09 *Left*. Reverse of the early Earl carte-de-visite FE06 numbered 3968. (WA)

FE10 *Below*. Earl had an extensive range of stereoscopic views on sale. This example shows the ruins of the Guesten Hall to the rear of the Cathedral. Guesten Hall was dismantled around 1860 (the roof being used for the Holy Trinity church at Shrub Hill) so this view would appear to date from around 1875.

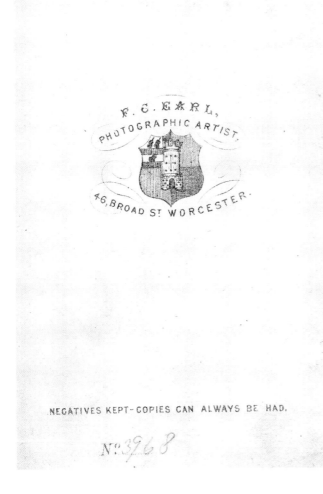

FE11 Carte-de-visite of Thomas Amphlett numbered 9958. He was born in 1859 and died in 1930. (WA)

FE12 Carte-de-visite of Harriet Amphlett numbered 9992. She was born in 1819 and died in 1880. She is posed looking through examples of Earl's work. (WA)

FE13 An unidentified carte-de-visite using the 'autotype patent'. The negative was especially suited to produce enlarged copies. Numbered 60,890 and dates from around 1883.

FE14 The grave of Catherine Maunsell on a fascinating carte-de-visite numbered 526. She died in the Upton-upon-Severn area in 1864 at the age of 76 but I have yet to identify the church in the background. She may have been buried in Ireland as she was the daughter of William Hare, the Earl of Listowel. Her late husband was Richard Maunsell K.C.

Earl was responsible for most of the cartes-de-visite that featured local views. They are difficult to find and I currently possess only a few examples. Another example of Earl's landscape cartes-de-visite can be found on page 88 of *Unseen Worcester* (No. 176 - Hardwick Court).

FE15 *Above.* The busy South Quay as seen from Bromwich Parade around 1880.

FE16 *Below.* Foregate Street looking northwards from the railway bridge. The bridge was built around 1860.

THE CROSS, WORCESTER.   Earl's Series, No. 60.

FE17 & FE18 Examples of Earl's postcard series. Earl was over 70 years old when the Edwardian craze for picture postcards was taking hold of the nation. He showed great enterprise, however, by publishing his own series of local non-photographic views. The card published as No. 1 is of Ombersley (see back cover) while the highest numbered I have seen so far is No. 105. I have seen only nineteen different examples so far, so the cards are fairly elusive (7 of Ombersley, 3 of Witley Court, 3 of Holt Fleet, 5 of Worcester and 1 of Salwarpe Court). Three of the cards are coloured (see back cover for examples) while thirteen have been postally used between August 15th 1902 and November 20th 1903 (shortly before the death of Earl).

OMBERSLEY, WORCESTERSHIRE.

EMPIRE STUDIOS

Empire Studios were initially based at 4 Bridge Street, Worcester and were probably primarily studio photographers. However, their proximity to the steamer moorings may have led them into specialising in photographs of the day trippers (many examples of these still exist today). Two of their much rarer aviation photographs can be seen in *Unseen Worcester* (Nos. 53 & 55 on pages 31/2). They also had branches at Oxford Chambers, Kidderminster, 164 High Street, Dudley and Lipton Chambers, Gloucester.

ES01 The Holt Castle near Holt Fleet bridge. In the background is a sign for the Wharf Hotel.

ES02 The Sabrina pulls alongside the Active. The view is looking south towards Diglis.

The proprietors of the Empire Studios were named Homer and were possibly brothers. Elijah James Homer was running the Dudley studio in 1912 but subsequently moved to Worcester (see page 155), while Edward James Homer was at Bridge Street in 1912, moving to 57 Foregate Street by 1915. The studio made occasional contributions to the *Berrow's Illustrated Supplement* between 1912 and 1921. Henry Iliffe probably took over the studio for a short period as he is listed at the Empire Studio, 60 Foregate Street in 1922.

ES03 & ES04 Two typical examples of the work of the Empire Studios. Both photographs were taken near Worcester bridge.

GEORGE EVANS

George Evans, one of six children, was born around 1823. His father, Matthew, was a school teacher while his mother, Emily, was a gloveress. They lived in the Blockhouse area of Worcester and George initially worked as a china potter at the nearby works of George Grainger. George worked from his home at Willow Place, Cromwell Street from around 1866 and was still listed in the local directories when he died in late 1903. He was married to Emma and they had three children (Charles, George and Jane). Jane worked for her father in the business. He often referred to his studio as being at 'Tallow Hill' or 'opposite the Vulcan Works'.

His work could be variable but was often of the highest quality as can be seen by the examples shown here. His cartes-de-visite and cabinet cards are un-numbered. A hand coloured Evans carte-de-visite can be seen on the back cover. The *Littlebury's Directory* for 1873 has an advertisement for Evans:

'Portrait, Architectural, and Landscape Photographer
Willow Place, Cromwell Street (near Shrub Hill railway station)
Every description of portrait from locket to life-size.'

GE01 *Above.* A George Evans carte-de-visite featuring George Evans.
GE02 *Below left.* A George Evans cabinet card featuring George Evans in later years.
GE03 *Below.* A cabinet card featuring George Evans, his son, Charles (a carpenter) and his daughter, Jane. Many thanks to the Evans family for the late inclusion in this book of the photographs on this page.

GE04 Early carte-de-visite of an unknown couple.

GE05 Charles Gardner, solicitor, of Ombersley. He was born in 1822 and died in 1887. (WA)

GE06 Early carte-de-visite of an unknown young man sat at a very ornate desk.

GE07 Carte-de-visite of an unknown girl.

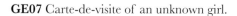

MAX FISCHER

Max Fischer operated initially from 33 Lowesmoor. He was listed in *Littlebury's Directory* for 1908 as a commercial printer (he was also featured in the *Worcester Daily Times Trade & Industrial Edition* of 1903 which mentioned his modern printing equipment) so it was perhaps not surprising that he turned his hand to photography. He had moved to 10 Barbourne Road by September 1911 where he continued his business activities. By 1930 he was listed as a wireless dealer so perhaps photography was no longer a service he offered. His name does not appear in the *Kelly's Directory* for 1940. His contributions to the *Berrow's Illustrated Supplement* started in June 1909 and covered a variety of local events including the Madresfield Territorial camp, Crowle point-to-point, hop picking at Holt, and the demolition of the Bell Hotel in 1913. His contributions reached a peak around 1912 and he continued to feature as a contributor into the 1920s.

MAX. FISCHER,

—Architectural and— Press Photographer.

HIGH SPEED WORK A SPECIALITY.

Commissions to cover Pictorial Newspaper Work in the County promptly attended to on receipt of wire.

LOCAL INCIDENTS KEPT UP TO DATE.

10, Barbourne Road, Worcester.

Photos by]   (1) THE CLUB HOUSE.   [Max. Fischer.
(2) THE THIRD GREEN.

Photo by]   THE LADIES' CLUB HOUSE.   [Max. Fischer

Fischer was commissioned to provide the photographs for the Worcester City Golf Club booklet of 1916. He used the booklet as an opportunity to advertise his services.
MF01 *Above left.* Fischer's full page advertisement.
MF02 *Above right.* Views of the golf course at Tolladine.
MF03 *Left.* The ladies club house.

MF04 The advertising photograph used by Fischer in the golf booklet helped to clarify that Fischer was the photographer of the above postcard which, I believe, shows the aircraft of Colonel Cody, the renowned American flyer, at Pitchcroft in August 1911 (a further example is photograph No. 52 on page 30 of *Unseen Worcester*).

MF05 Fischer evidently took a series of photographs at the Unionist Fete of 1913 where Lord and Lady Coventry viewed the flying demonstrations. This postcard features the embossed signature of Max Fischer in the bottom right-hand corner. Unfortunately, Fischer used embossed cards intermittently. His work is a mixture of embossed signature, reverse side printing of his name & address, or no identification whatsoever.

Two further examples of Fischer's superb series which unfortunately are rare and elusive items to find. Both postcards were postally used in 1910. Other probable examples of this series can be found in *Unseen Worcester* on pages 41 and 43 (Nos. 74, 78 and 79). Research into this series is still on-going.

MF13 *Above.* Vernon Park, Malvern Road.
MF14 *Below.* Comer Road, St. John's.

MF15 Shepherds Conference procession at The Cross, Worcester. The banner is that of the Ashton Unity. Featured in the *Berrow's Illustrated Supplement* of June 5th 1914.

MF16 Goulding's Central Committee Rooms in Foregate Street were a hive of activity as election day (probably the general election of 1910) approached. The posters concern free trade and tariff reform.

MF17 Holes and Smith before a fierce bout. Featured in the *Berrow's Illustrated Supplement* of April 4th 1914.

MF18 A rare interior view of a public house possibly in the Rainbow Hill area of Worcester. Postcard postally used on February 6th 1918.

Fischer visited many events in and around Worcester. Unfortunately he did not always pinpoint the events depicted and a fair amount of detective work has been necessary in order to identify accurately his work.

MF19 *Above.* The Co-operative Society's Children's Gala that featured in the *Berrow's Illustrated Supplement* of July 15th 1911. It was probably held at Perdiswell.

MF20 *Below.* The Brotherhood Fete of 1913 which was held in the grounds of St. Catherine's Hill, London Road, Worcester (also see page 37). Another scene of the event appears in the *Berrow's Illustrated Supplement* of August 9th 1913.

MF21 St. Mary's Band of Hope Concert - 'The Teasing Tea Party'. This was featured in the *Berrow's Illustrated Supplement* of December 24th 1910. St. Mary's church has now been converted into apartments.

MF22 Both Clutterbuck (see CL14 on page 31) and Fischer made their way to the flooded Hylton Road in December 1910 to capture the impact of the floods on local people. This fine photographic postcard shows the premises of G. Yeates, potato and fruit merchant. The factory in the distance is that of the Severn Bank Tannery. My great aunt, Emily Jones, worked there at one time; she lived close by in Chequers Lane. The man in the boat holding the punt was Charles Webb, a waterman, who lived at 131 Hylton Road. He was renowned for always coming to the rescue of his distressed neighbours during the occasional floods. His wife, Hannah, was a glove maker.

CROWN EAST FETE, 1909.

MF23 Fischer took a series of photographs at the Crown East Fete of July 1909. This photograph, coupled with a similar photograph, was one of his earliest contributions to the *Berrow's Illustrated Supplement* .

MF24 Fischer travelled fair distances during the course of his work. This is the Feckenham Horticultural Show that featured in the *Berrow's Illustrated Supplement* of September 14th 1912.

FOX & COMPANY

John Edward Fox took over the studios occupied by A. & G. Taylor at 37 The Tything around 1888. From 1890 onwards the business was trading as J. H. Fox & Co. and they had branches locally at Unicorn Hill, Redditch (around 1887-96) and Kidderminster. Further afield they had branches in Birmingham, Coventry and Leicester so were essentially multi-branch photographers. During the late 1890s onwards the business was run by three people: Harry Proud, the manager who was, apparently, rather pompous; Mr Pepper, who did the processing, printing, artistry, and hand colouring; and the photographer, Bertie Dinsdale. Their main contract was with the nearby prison in Castle Street (which closed around 1922) as all inmates had to be photographed. They were perhaps never the most prosperous of businesses and the outbreak of the First World War (which inevitably made it difficult to obtain chemical supplies etc.) did them no favours. The increasing competition from better financed and larger multi-branch photographers was an increasing problem now the Great War was over and business from the prison was decreasing. They appear to have ceased trading around 1919. Bertie Dinsdale then became a freelance photographer (see page 49).

FX01 Detail from a cabinet card showing the ornate monogram used by Fox and Company which comprised the letters from 'J.H.F. & Co.'. The Redditch studio developed a different version utilizing the letters of their manager's name (HC = Harry Coles).

FX02 A cabinet card with the names, Frank and Alice, inscribed on the reverse.

FX03 The reverse side of a cabinet card.

37, Tything, Worcester,   *April 28ᵗʰ 1905*

Mrs Woodhouse

Dr to J. H. Fox & Co.

Artists & Photographers.

ENLARGEMENTS TO ANY SIZE IN OILS, WATER AND CARBON.

	£	s	d
To 1/2 doz Cabinets grp & reorder		7	6

Recd by subscriptions
J H Fox & Co
per EP

With thanks

FOX04 Fox & Co. receipt. Cabinet photographs were priced at 7 shillings 6 pence for six or 14 shillings 6 pence for twelve. These were fairly expensive items for the average Edwardian family so they were often paid for by a subscription fund. (ED)

FOX06 Detail of the reverse of a Fox & Co. receipt for payments. The funding of photographs was a relatively complex process for the ordinary Edwardian family. (ED)

FOX05 Detail of the front of a Fox & Co. receipt for payments. (ED)

Date *May 9/04*   No. **11576**

J. H. FOX & Co.,

Artists and Photographers,

Enlargements to any size in Oils, Water, and Carbon,

37, TYTHING, WORCESTER

Received _____ of Mr _____

Address _____

on account of _____

value _____

Canvasser _____

Future payments to be made to the Collector, who must give a Printed Coupon Receipt for all payments after this date.

EBENR. BAYLIS & SON, WORCESTER.

☙ NOTICE. ❧

Should the Collector neglect calling two weeks running, please to report at office without delay.

Originals of any value must be given in at the office.

Proofs for orders over 5/- are sent for approval, and should they not be satisfactory (through the expression or dress, &c.), a Re-sitting will be given and fresh proof sent for a nominal payment of One Shilling for Carte, or Two Shillings for Cabinet Negative.

Enlargements can be made from any Negative Photograph or Picture in good preservation, but no Cartes or Cabinets can be given, as extra care and work is caused in finishing.

Coupons &c. must be taken care of, and given up at the completion of contract, and available only for twelve months after date of issue.

Signed J. H. FOX & CO.

WALTER W. HARRIS

Walter W. Harris was a pianoforte, music dealer and photographer of *Cecilia House* 101 High Street. The music business dated back to 1790. His stock of musical and photographic items occupied four floors of the premises. He specialised in local views and boasted in 1903 that he had the most complete and select collection of photographs in the Worcester area. This statement cannot be verified for certain but much of his work still survives today. It seems probable that many of the postcards published by Harris were also photographed by him personally but it is possible that he employed other photographers as his views encompassed areas as far away as Evesham, Broadway and Storridge. His photographic postcards are a strange mixture of the animated and dull variety. The views that lack human presence are almost too good to be true. He appeared to be a member of the Cathedral Choir and he was active in religious circles. Consequently much of his work has a religious bias and his coverage of postcard views of Worcestershire churches was second to none. He was featured in the *Worcester Daily Times Trade & Industrial Edition* of 1903 which praised his recent photographs of the architectural beauties of the Cathedral.

WH01 The premises of W.W. Harris around 1896. Postcards were still a phenomenon largely waiting to happen in the United Kingdom in 1896 so Walter's display is bereft of postcard views (the earliest known postally used Worcester postcard is dated 5th June 1899; Scarborough, however, has a postcard sent in 1894). There are, however, a number of photographic items on display. (WRO)

WH02 A close up view of the Harris shopfront reveals the variety of photographic items he had for sale. (WRO)

WH03 Worcester Cathedral Voluntary Choir at Stratford, July 28th 1919. This was probably their annual outing. Postcard sent by Harris personally. This photograph also appeared in the *Berrow's Illustrated Supplement*.

WH04 *Above.* The Cenotaph within the grounds of the Cathedral. It was built in 1919.

WH05 & WH06 *Left & below.* The lifting and moving of the Trinity House took place in 1891 which was several years before the publication of these postcards (see JC01 on page 22).

87

WH07 *Above.* Worcester Tank Bank Week held March 17th-24th 1918 in the grounds of the Cathedral. On page 101 there is a photograph by Iliffe featuring fund raisers by the tank (HI01).

WH09, WH10, WH11 & WH12 *Opposite page, right.* Photographic postcard views of the secondary streets around the city centre are virtually non-existent so these views of Lich Street, New Street, Birdport (below photograph of Lich Street) and Copenhagen Street (then Fish Street) are rare items. These photographs, taken around 1904, show that Worcester had the undoubted potential to now be a tourist attraction as popular as York or Bath. I know that these scenes have been published previously but feel it is important to show them together as an appreciation of Harris's work.

WH08 *Below.* Laslett's Almshouses, on the corner of Friar Street and Union Street, pictured in 1912.

LichStreet. Worcester.

New Street. Worcester

WH13 Guildhall celebrations. Did Harris use a platform in order to take this view? It was more probably taken from an upper floor window on the eastern side of High Street.

WH14 A rare photographic postcard showing part of the city wall and part of the bastion of Sidbury Gate that was revealed when excavations took place in Sidbury in May 1907.

WH15 St. George's church, Worcester, around 1908

WH16 Court Farm, Himbleton around 1908.

Harris produced many Edwardian views of the Spetchley area. Interestingly many of these postcards were not postally used so may have been bought principally as mementos. They were certainly not printed with the aim of high usage by the inhabitants of Spetchley which only had a population of 118 in 1901.

WH17 *Above.* Spetchley Hall around 1906. The home of the Berkeley family.
WH18 *Below.* Round Hill was the residence of Reverend Norman Holly in 1912. The Round Hill is a circular elevation nearby.

WH19 & WH20 Harris had an extensive coverage of Worcestershire views. I am not aware of any other Worcester based Edwardian photographer who regularly strayed as far as Inkberrow or Abbots Morton (the Abbots Morton postcard was postally used in 1907).

WH21 Picturesque Cropthorne evidently attracted two photographers on the same day! Unfortunately I can shed no light on the identity of our mystery photographer.

WH22 Earls Croome Court which came up for sale recently. Only of interest to the wealthy I am afraid!

WH23 & WH24 Harris also had views to sell of the far west of the county, even venturing as far as Suckley and Storridge.

WH25 & WH26 Witley Court and church were often subjects for the local photographer. Harris was one of many photographers who travelled to Witley for work. Others included Wedley of Stourport and White of Kidderminster.

Witley Court.

WH27 & WH28 Fine views of Witley Court but curiously they lack any human presence. Perhaps Harris was especially commissioned to take a series of views of Witley Court and church. The photographs on pages 96 and 97 probably date from around 1903.

WH29 Martley Rectory around 1908.

WH30 A rare view of hop drying at Shelsley Walsh. The man second from the right is thought to be Roland Gwinnet.

WH31 Westwood House still lies in a beautiful setting close to the ever growing urban mass of Droitwich.

WH32 A rare interior view of the hall in Westwood House which is now split into various apartments.

WH33 Cottages in Sinton Lane, Ombersley that were rebuilt in 1839. Unbelievably, these cottages were demolished in the early 1970s in order to make way for the current bypass.

WH34 Camp Lock, Grimley. This is still an attractive place to visit on warm summer evenings when a glass of scrumpy at the nearby Camp hostelry goes down rather well!

HENRY ILIFFE

Henry Iliffe took over the studios of Frederick Whaley at 38 High Street, Worcester around 1910. He then moved to 57 The Tything (taking over the studios of Terry & Fryer) around 1912. J. Parkes Foy had taken over the studio by 1921 with Iliffe then being listed at the Empire Studio, 60 Foregate Street (1922). He had disappeared from the directories by 1924 while his occasional contributions to the *Berrow's Illustrated Supplement* had ceased in 1919.

HI01 Fund raisers for Tank Bank Week which was held in the grounds of the Cathedral (March 17th-24th 1918).

HI02 The choir outside Powick church in 1919.

HI03 Iliffe took photographs of amateur performers at the Theatre Royal. This is Leslie W. Moore playing Sir Walter Blount in April 1914.

HI04 A studio portrait of a young girl.

HI06 A studio portrait of a young boy.

HI05 Edward Lamb in his RAMC uniform.

MAXTON

Maxton was based in Kempsey and perhaps was mainly an enthusiastic amateur. His photographs, however, reveal a great ability to capture a moment in time with panache. He was operating around 1906-1916.

MX01 & MX02
Above left and right. Two charming photographs of local children.

MX03 The floods of August 1912.

MX04 A superb snow scene in Kempsey. On the right is the Talbot Hotel.

MX05 'Icicles at Kempsey' is the caption to this postcard. The thatched cottage was at Bannut Hill (see PP36 on page 124) and, according to the writer, was roughly opposite *The Lawns* which, at that time around 1912, was the residence of Mrs Wynter.

ARTHUR J. NEALE

Arthur J. Neale, who was deaf, worked full-time at the Royal Porcelain Works and was also designated Works Photographer but his employers allowed him to operate his own photographic studio, which was situated at his home at *Braemar* 96 Bath Road (from around 1905 to 1933), in order to supplement his income. Harry Davis, the famous porcelain painter, recalled that Neale's wages at that time were all of £1 out of which 2 shillings superannuation was stopped. Neale made occasional contributions to the *Berrow's Illustrated Supplement* including the Worcester Rifle Club at Tiddesley Wood (June 5th 1909), Mr H.W. Adams in his art studio (March 26th 1910), and a rare image of the renowned late George Owen, who had spent 55 years of his life at the Royal Porcelain Works, at his potters wheel (February 1917). Neale continued to be a photographer until his death in January 1933 at the relatively early age of 61. He had been employed at the porcelain works for over 40 years. He had been well known in Conservative and Oddfellow circles and was Honorary Treasurer of the Midland Counties' Institute for the Deaf. Harry Davis was among the mourners at his funeral.

AN01 Arthur J. Neale. In his younger days he had been a keen cyclist and gymnast. He was still a member of the St. John's Cycling Club at the time of his death. (JH)

AN02 A prize won in the countryside. Perhaps to do with angling or shooting. Other photographs that Neale took may be found in *Porcelain in Worcester* (No. 91 - Howard Hadley, No. 127 - Josiah Davis, and No. 145 - Royal Porcelain Works Cycling Club). No. 148 on page 86 in *Porcelain in Worcester* shows a Neale advertisement.

J. PARKES FOY

J. Parkes Foy replaced Henry Iliffe at 57 The Tything around 1920. He was still operating from there when the Second World War broke out. Geoffrey Hopcraft was to take over the business but retained the trading name of Foy as late as 1956.

PF01 Young Worcester Rowing Club members with an array of trophies. Edward Lamb is sitting down on the right-hand side (see HI05 on page 102).

PF02 A Worcester Royal Grammar School cricket team at Flagge Meadow.

PP12 A superb social history study - possibly church missionaries or the like visiting gypsies in the Worcestershire countryside. The caravan on the left was made by Smith of Birmingham.

PP13 A more wealthy form of transport! I wonder if anyone knows who this relatively wealthy couple were?

Unidentified personnel and unidentified scenes but superb examples of local social history.

PP14 *Above.* A real photographic snow scene captioned 'The cottage'. But which cottage and where during the late snow of
April 15th 1921?
PP15 *Below.* Comfortable horse-drawn transport?

Like Colwell, Parsons took many photographs in the hop fields. Unfortunately very few hop field and hop yard photographs were positively identified by the individual photographers. The location of PP16 and PP17 is, as is usual, unknown.

PP16 *Above.* A typical scene with hops being deposited in a crib. The young lad holding the basket also appears in PP17.

PP17 *Below.* An unusual view of a mechanical device that was probably used for pressing hops.

PP18 The road to Suckley and Smith End Green. Looking northwards from the main road through Leigh Sinton.

PP19 Sarah Banner stands in the doorway of the Leigh Sinton premises of Banner & Son - coach builders, wheelwrights & general smiths. Photograph No. 187 in my book *Unseen Worcester* (also taken by Parsons) shows a wedding party outside what appeared to be a public house but in fact it was the Banner household and featured the wedding of Thomas Henry Jones & Gladys Elizabeth Mary Banner on April 22nd 1914. The wedding photograph was featured in the *Berrow's Illustrated Supplement* on May 9th 1914.

PP20 A superb rural study of Leigh Post Office. A very early embossed real photographic postcard which was postally used in May 1905.

PP21 A general view of Leigh showing the post office in the middle distance.

PP22 The station at Leigh Court was situated on the Worcester - Bromyard - Leominster branch line. Like photograph PP20 also postally used from Leigh in 1905 and it would seem likely that Leigh Post Office stocked a small range of Parsons real photographic postcards.

PP23 Parsons used his own postcards to inform his customers of intended visits. The Hammond family were previous customers of Parsons. The Hammond family also feature on page 58 (HD03).

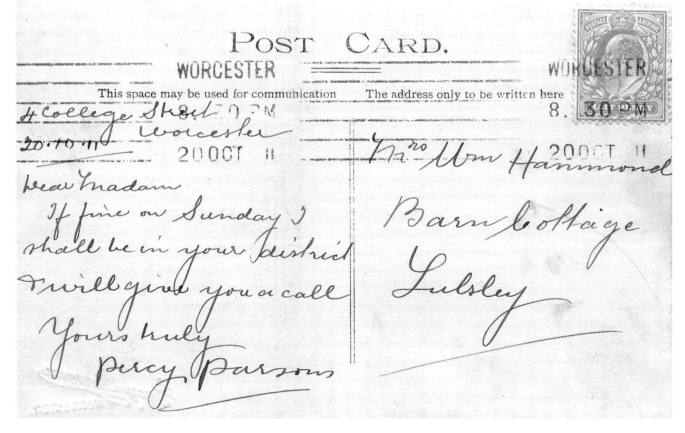

PP24 *Above left.* A carte-de-visite of Hammond family members that dates from around 1902.

PP25, PP26 & PP27 *Above right & below.* Three postcards of the Hammond household from Parsons' visit of October 1911.

PP28 Church Lane, Broadheath as seen from the Worcester to Martley road. On the right is the village hall, while in the far right distance is the vicarage.

PP29 The Worcester to Martley road, Broadheath with the nurseries on the right. Postcard postally used in 1921.

Percy Parsons made many trips to & through Hallow. I have seen at least twenty different Parsons' views of Hallow.
PP30 *Above.* This 1905 view of the Green is from one of his early trips.
PP31 *Below.* A later trip showing the school on the left.

HALLOW

PP32 The main road through Shrawley. Parsons often took photographs in this area.

PP33 The Half Way House, Dunhampton. The licensee was E. Oakley.

PP42 The post office at Fernhill Heath around 1920. No need for speed limits then!

PP43 Ombersley Road looking northwards towards the junction with Checketts Lane. Obviously not a rush hour view!

PP44 A fine view of Gheluvelt Park. Postally used in 1927.

PP45 Kepax Ferry on a postcard personally used by Parsons on 26th February 1929. Percy wrote to a jeweller friend in London: 'The watch safely to hand' ....'frost sharp last night, and snowing all day'.

PP46 & PP47 Bromwich House was once set in very extensive grounds. A much changed scene today although the house still survives amidst urban mayhem on the busy Bromwich Road.

PP48 The Capital and Counties Bank on the corner of High Street and Bank Street. The postcard was postally used on 29th July 1908.

PP49 A fine array of workmen with their horses. I am fairly certain that this photograph was taken at the Worcester Corporation Stores situated in The Butts. Can anyone verify this for me?

PP50 The Amalgamated Society of Railway Servants held a Church Parade at Tewkesbury on August 27th 1911. This is the Worcester banner. I am not certain of the location.

PP51 The Great Western Railway Sheet Department float at a Pitchcroft Fete.

PP52 A Worcester police contingent outside the Cathedral. They were on Three Choirs Festival duties. At the centre of the front row is Inspector F.W. Peacock. Other policemen included Inspector Bishop, Sergeants Mound, Miller and Steadman, detectives Bradley and Deakin, and PCs Lewis, Jauncey, Price, Pitt, Penlington, Tomlinson, Bailey, Brotherton, Hollis, Lock, Evans, Sparkes, Fennell, Repton and Gregg.

PP53 A police inspection at the rear of a hall in Silver Street. The buildings in the background appear to be those of the Hill Evans vinegar works so this would be the eastern side of Silver Street I presume. Inspector Bishop is highlighted and he also appears in PP52 - he is obviously the one with the moustache!

The next series of postcards by Parsons show his work at its best - capturing in full the election fever of early February 1908 Some background history will help an understanding of the historical significance of the following photographs:

The Liberals, led by sitting minority Prime Minister Henry Campbell-Bannerman, had won a large majority in the 1906 general election. The Conservatives under Arthur Balfour lost more than half their seats (not including Worcester which had elected George Henry Williamson), while the Labour Representation Committee was far more successful than in 1900 and after the election was reformed as 'The Labour Party' with 29 MPs and Keir Hardie as leader. The Irish Parliamentary Party, led by John Redmond, achieved its seats with a relatively low number of votes, as 74 candidates stood unopposed.

The primary reason given by historians for the Conservative Party's landslide defeat was the party's weakness after its split over the issue of free trade (Joseph Chamberlain had resigned from government in September 1903 in order to campaign for tariff reform, which would allow 'preferential tariffs'). Many working class people saw this as a threat to the price of food, hence the debate was nicknamed 'Big Loaf, Little Loaf'. The Liberals landslide victory led to the passing of social legislation known as the Liberal reforms.

A by-election became necessary at Worcester in early 1908 and the two candidates were Mr Edward Goulding (Conservative) and Mr Harold Elverston (Liberal). Tariff reform was still the item highest on the political agenda but the suffragette movement was also to play a role in local politics; by-elections in Mid-Devon and South Herefordshire had given the suffragettes the opportunity to push their cause and now Worcester was the focus of their efforts. According to the *Worcester Journal* of February 1st 1908 there were two suffragist organizations: one was the National Women's Social and Political Union (NWSPU) which opposed the Liberal government (in militant ways) while the other was the National Union of Women's Suffrage Societies (NUWSS) which contented itself with supporting any individual member of parliament who favoured the enfranchisement of women.

This was, however, to ignore the recently formed Women's Freedom League: in 1907 some leading members of the NWSPU had begun to question the leadership of Emmeline Pankhurst and Christabel Pankhurst. These women objected to the way that the Pankhursts were making decisions without consulting members. They also felt that a small group of wealthy women like Emmeline Pethick-Lawrence were having too much influence over the organisation. In the autumn of 1907, Teresa Billington-Greig, Elizabeth How-Martyn, Dora Marsden, Margaret Nevinson, Charlotte Despard and about seventy other members of the NWSPU left to form the Women's Freedom League (WFL). Like the NWSPU, the Women's Freedom League was a militant organisation that was willing the break the law. As a result, over 100 of their members were sent to prison after being arrested on demonstrations (including members chaining themselves to objects in the Houses of Parliament) or refusing to pay taxes. However the WFL was a completely non-violent organisation and opposed the NWSPU campaign of vandalism against private and commercial property. The WFL were especially critical of the NWSPU arson campaign. The WFL grew to over 4,000 members and published *The Vote* newspaper.

All three organizations made their presence felt during the Worcester election campaign:

a/ The NWSPU held a frenetic and densely packed meeting in the Hopmarket Hotel yard using a dray as their main platform. Miss Keevil (a prominent suffragette) introduced the speakers that included Emmeline Pankhurst. Pankhurst had, apparently, been injured by being rolled in the mud by unhappy and incensed Liberals in Mid-Devon where the suffragettes campaigning had helped to result in a Liberal loss to the Conservatives. This did not deter her presence at Worcester, however, where she attacked the Liberals vigorously: when reminded by a member of the audience that Elverston had stated that he was in favour of votes for women she retorted that he should not be a candidate in support of a government that opposed women's suffrage.

b/ The NUWSS held a well attended meeting at their rooms in Foregate Street where Mrs Wilson (wife of Canon Wilson of Worcester) gave an address to an audience of mainly working people.

c/ The WFL obtained temporary campaign rooms at Arboretum House in Arboretum Road and showed the citizens of Worcester what pro-active campaigners they were. Their actions were not reported by the press as far as I am aware but, fortunately, the intrepid Percy Parsons did not ignore their feisty and significant presence.

PP54 Members of the WFL writing slogans and advertising their meetings in chalk on the pavements of East Street situated in the Arboretum. In the background is their Arboretum House base. Placards in favour of Goulding are also visible.

PP55 The WFL, having completed their chalking, don billboards that espouse their cause in various different ways. It is unlikely that they were local women; they were probably major members of the WFL. Possibly among them was Emma Lloyd Sproson, a prominent West Bromwich born suffragette who had just helped to open a branch of the WFL at Wolverhampton.

PP56 A cab load of suffragettes outside Arboretum House which was then an apartment block. It would be interesting to know if this was election day and whether the suffragettes took part in the election processions. They were definitely in favour of Goulding and fervently anti Elverston, the Liberal candidate.

PP57 Goulding supporters in high spirits. They believed that a vote for the Conservatives would result in more work and food. Note the loaves on sticks. The location could well be Angel Street as the premises behind has posters proclaiming offices to let that mention T.J. Stephens of 5 Angel Street. Furthermore, the licensee of the Fountain Inn at 11 Angel Street in 1908 was Edward Price while Stephens was in situ at 9 Angel Street.

PP58 On board the donkey cart are a lady and a man disguised as a lady. There is possibly a suffragette connotation here. The location is probably College Street, near to the Cathedral (see PP59).

Suffragism in 1908 was still subject to contempt, hostility and bewilderment but maybe the patronising attitude of their erstwhile supporters was difficult to bear too; I am not sure how much Goulding appreciated the support of the suffragettes. He had a slightly condescending attitude towards them as revealed by this extract from one of his speeches: 'he had always been captivated by the ladies, though he had not actually been captured by them yet' (laughter and loud applause). 'He had always been faithful to them' (laughter). 'He had always voted for them and it was twenty years since he gave his first vote in favour of women's right to vote, and he had seen no reason, from that day to this, to change his opinion'.

Goulding mainly campaigned on tariff reform and this was the main issue for the people of Worcester: more food and more work was what they wanted. Suffragism was almost a novelty distraction but nevertheless the foundations of support for women's right to vote was being laid in Worcester in early 1908. The *Worcester Herald* commented that the suffragettes were 'led by ladies of marked ability, who had done their best to ruffle the placid surface and have to some extent succeeded'.

Goulding duly won the election; he polled 4,361 votes to Elverston's 3,069. He made his celebratory speech from the balcony of the Star Hotel in Foregate Street. The suffragettes had achieved their task in Worcester in keeping the Liberals out. Goulding also contested the seat successfully in the 1910 general election, albeit with a slightly reduced majority. The Liberals nationally, however, just managed to cling on to power in 1910. This was not the result the suffragettes had wanted and their aim for the right to vote still seemed a distant possibility at the end of the Edwardian era.

PP59 The donkey cart is dwarfed by a cab load of local dignitaries. It appears the election procession started near the Cathedral and terminated in Foregate Street, close to the committee rooms of both candidates. The premises to the right is that of Richard Haughton, a monumental sculptor, at 33 College Street.

STAFFORD HARDING

Stafford Harding traded from the 'Little Wonderland' studio at 4 Friar Street. I have only seen three examples of his work. He is listed in the local directories as a shopkeeper between 1921-1936. His photograph of Stoulton Football Club appeared in the *Berrow's Illustrated Supplement* of October 29th 1921.

SH01 Young boys at Worcester quay around 1920.

SH02 Sarah Stockton pictured in hop fields near Worcester. She was born around 1873 and married Robert Orgee, a brush finisher of Worcester, around 1890. They lived in a crowded court in Copenhagen Street, Worcester and had eight children. Hop picking was an ideal way for them to supplement their meagre income. Sarah was my great grandmother. The Stocktons were fairground people and tracing their family history is no easy task!

JAMES H. STEWART

James Hunter Stewart was based initially at Sansome Walk (around 1867) and then at Chestnut Walk from 1868. This was the last reference to Stewart in the local directories.

JHS01 & JHS02 Front & reverse of a carte-de-visite of Lilian Boucher (or Bougher?) pictured in 1868. This carte-de-visite was hand coloured (see back cover).

JHS03 A carte-de-visite of an unknown gentleman. The reverse design is identical to that of JHS02.

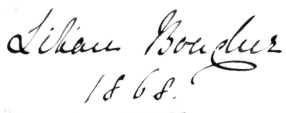

HUBERT A. STRETTON

Hubert Stretton was based at the Barbourne Studio - 41 Barbourne Road, Worcester around 1915-16. He probably previously operated from his home at 302 Ombersley Road. On April 14th 1914 he submitted a photograph of Augustus Stretton, 'a well-known Worcester citizen', to the *Berrow's Illustrated Supplement*. His work is not easy to find and I have currently seen less than ten examples of his photographs. Photograph HS04 features the Plough at Tibberton and can be found opposite the contents page.

Two postcards of Stretton that emanated from the same source.
HS01 *Above.* Relatives of Frederick Howell on a rural jaunt.
HS02 *Left.* Frederick Howell on 'Jacky' in April 1917.

HS03 An unidentified house, probably in Britannia Square.

WILLIAM WILKINS

William Wilkins was initially based at his home at *Kent Cottage* 106 Bromyard Road, Worcester (around 1908-1915). He then moved to 74 Northwick Road, Worcester. As well as producing postcards he took family photographs including the Bertie Dinsdale family. He was also responsible for a series of back street postcard views (see WW03). My knowledge of this series is, as yet, scant. Wilkins did not always sign his work so he may be responsible for more of the local output of photographs than the coverage he receives here. Research is on-going. He made occasional contributions to the *Berrow's Illustrated Supplement* including the new Ham bridge on February 27th 1909, sheep shearing at Holt on June 25th 1910, a children's fishing contest at Kempsey on August 19th 1922 and Hallow Football Club on March 17th 1923. Like many of the lesser known photographers he found it difficult to compete with the up-and-coming multi-branch photographers who had more modern and advanced equipment.

WW01 *Right.* A patient at Knightwick Sanatorium on January 27th 1926.

WW02 The Dinsdale family photographed by Wilkins in his Northwick Road back garden on September 5th 1926. Back row, left to right: May, Amelia, Albert, Mary. Front row: George, Irene, Bertie (the photographer), Howard, May (Bertie's wife), Ethel (baby), Doris and Cecil. This family of ten was still not complete; three more children were to be born - girl twins in 1928 (Joyce and Gladys) and another boy in 1931 (Eugene). They feature in photograph HD07 on page 59.

R. BROOKSBANK

R. Brooksbank was based at 19 Silver Street, Worcester from around 1860-1868. Examples of his work are difficult to find.

OP04 The reverse of this carte-de-visite shows that Brooksbank took over at Silver Street from A. Brandish.

E. COXELL

Edwin Coxell was based at 6 College Street, Worcester from around 1872-1874. Examples of his work are also difficult to find.

OP05 Carte-de-visite studio study of an unknown lady.

F. DOWNING

Frederick Downing was based at *Holland Villas* 21 Ombersley Road according to *Littlebury's Directory* for 1908. The *Kelly's Directory* for 1904 lists a Benjamin Williams, photographer, at this address so there may have been a studio in situ when Downing moved in. Downing is then listed in the directories at 16 Edgar Street, Worcester (1910-1915). Examples of his work are difficult to find. He made a few contributions to the *Berrow's Illustrated Supplement* including one on July 2nd 1910.

OP06 A postcard of the Worcestershire Senior Cup.

J.S. GREEN

John Smith Green was yet another photographer to be based at 37 The Tything and was in situ from around 1882-1884. He was replaced by A. & G. Taylor by 1885.

OP07 Carte-de-visite of Thomas Edward Amphlett of Acton Hall. He was born in 1857 and died in 1942 so would have been aged about 26 when this photograph was taken. (WA)

37, TYTHING.
WORCESTER.

A.H. GUMMERY

Gummery lived at *The Larkins*, Highfields, Wichenford around 1912. He did not sign his work which makes research on his work difficult. I think he may be responsible for a series of views published by Mr. Hall at the Martley Post Office. He made occasional contributions to the *Berrow's Illustrated Supplement* from around 1910 onwards. These included a butter making class at Martley on May 28th 1910 and an accident to a horse and trap at Prickley Green on June 11th 1910. Research is ongoing.

OP08 The hounds at Deadfield Cover. Postcard personally sent by Gummery to Mr Browning at the Wharf Hotel, Holt Fleet in February 1912.

HEMMING BROS.

Hemming Brothers are not listed in the directories that I have consulted.

OP09 It is rare to find cartes-de-visite that emanate from rural sources. I have a similar item relating to E. Gaskin of Pensax.

E.J. HOMER

Elijah James Homer had been one of the proprietors of the Empire Studios. He then operated from his home at 60 Chestnut Walk, Worcester. He made many contributions to the *Berrow's Illustrated Supplement* from 1922 onwards. His work seems rather elusive in view of the many contributions he made so possibly he did not always acknowledge his work. However the reverse side of OP10 has a clear circular handstamp bearing the name and address of Homer.

OP10 Unfortunately I have no information concerning the location or date of this float that extols the virtues of visiting the Droitwich Brine Baths.

N. MAY

Norman May was also based at 37 The Tything and was probably the first studio owner at this address The studio only covered the ground floor of the premises. By 1879 he was in partnership with Stowe but the studio was to pass on to Ernest E. White in that same year. White had moved to Worcester from Reading where he had been in partnership with Sydney Victor. White, however, was only in situ until 1882 when John S. Green took over the studio. I have yet to see an example of White's work. May probably achieved greater success in Great Malvern where he was based initially at Gazebo House, Church Street (around 1879 - probably premises once used by Bennett), and then Priory Mount, Church Street from around 1881 (the studio as used by Francis Earl around 1873-1881). May was the official photographer to the Worcestershire Exhibition of 1882 (held at Shrub Hill, Worcester).

OP11 A rare carte-de-visite taken in the Worcestershire countryside featuring a rural worker.

NORMAN MAY,   WORCESTER.

MELBA STUDIOS

The Melba Studios were situated in the High Street, Worcester. They were probably a multi-branch operation as there was also a Melba Studio in Worcester Street, Kidderminster. I believe they were working as photographers during and around the Second World War.

OP12 Smartly uniformed young men pictured at Worcester's Melba Studios.

A. MERRIMAN

A. Merriman was based in Kempsey. His work is elusive but he did make occasional contributions to the *Berrow's Illustrated Supplement* including the arrival of hop pickers at Holt Fleet on September 25th 1909, a children's tea party at Holt vicarage on December 3rd 1910 and Napleton Grange cottage (Kempsey) - tiles being substituted for thatch - on December 3rd 1910.

OP13 A photograph possibly featuring a family from the Ombersley area.

E.J. MORLEY

Eric J. Morley was based at 20 and 21 St. Nicholas Street, Worcester from around 1884-1885. Percy Parsons was to take over his studio. He was apparently in partnership with Barwick at one time.

OP14 & OP15 Two rare Morley studio cartes-de-visite. They are undated and un-numbered.

MORLEY & BARWICK,   WORCESTER

ERIC MORLEY.   WORCESTER.

B. MORRIS

B. Morris occupied the old Earl studios at 46 Broad Street for a short period during the 1890s.

OP16 This cabinet card of Mabel is dated February 26th 1894.

W.E. PRICE

Wilfred Price was based in the Knightwick and Martley area in the post First World War period.

OP17 Hill Top, Knightwick which featured in Price's Real Photo Series.

A. & G. TAYLOR

Alexander and George Taylor were based at the former Earl studios at 46 Foregate Street around 1884 but soon moved premises to the much used studio at 37 The Tything. They were not in situ for long, however, being replaced by J.H. Fox & Co. (or possibly a John Edward Fox) by around 1888. A. & G. Taylor had branches in many locations throughout the country and were one of the first multi-branch photographic businesses. It is possible that J.H. Fox was their branch manager and that he subsequently took over the Worcester business. A. & G. Taylor held a Royal Warrant and their UK work is quite easy to find.

OP18 This A. & G. Taylor carte-de-visite was actually the work of the Worcester branch of Fox & Co. A case of using up existing stock or trading on the name of a well-known photographer?

A. & G. TAYLOR   PHOTOGRAPHERS TO THE QUEEN.

OP19 As a national company A. & G. Taylor produced an extensive 'Reality Series' of photographic postcards. This example probably dates from around 1904.